Raising Anxiety-Free Children In The 21st Century

By

Dr. H. M. Saleem, Ed.D.

A Parent Guide to Child Anxiety & Stress
And
What to Do About It Without Being Ashamed

Copyright

Cover design by: KEYNOTE 180

Published and Printed
in
The United States of America

Dedication

To my wife, Attia Saleem, and my three boys, Farhad, Khayyam, and Anbar Saleem whose lives have inspired me to share with other parents, who wish to raise their children free of all stresses and anxieties, whatever little success I had in raising my children.

Table of Contents

The Companion Website to This Book

There are many resources and video tutorials embedded throughout the digital version of this book. For the print version, we have created a special website. Please visit

www.keynote180.com/anxiety-free-children

Preface

One can safely predict the growth in Child Psychology will forever continue in spite of the tremendous body of work done by some of the greatest names in behavioral psychology. This prediction is based on the evolving nature of triggers that cause stress and anxiety in children. Technology and social media have altered the nature of relationships in ways that had never existed before. Your child's mood now swings with the number of 'likes' and 'emojis' on their Instagram or Snapchat. Facebook posts affect parents' temper and tenor with their children. Child psychology is still evolving to deal with social digital relationships. It has yet to deal with the impact of online learning on children's behavior. It has yet to deal with the effects of isolation imposed by pandemics.

This book is a teacher's and a parent's experience in dealing with child anxieties and behaviors under these circumstances. This is in no way an expert replacement of a professional psychologist's intervention in severe cases, but it does attempt to provide answers to most common situations of child anxiety and stress.

Dr. H. M. Saleem, Ed.D.

KEYNOTE 180 | Penguin House Inc.

dr.saleem@keynote180.com

Introduction

Jack was only 14, still in ninth grade, when his father died. He would often wake up at night crying, dead scared, not knowing who to ask for the answers to all the questions that were not letting him sleep. The question of where to get the money for the computer he needed for homework; the question of how to deal with that big bully in the school who kept harassing him; the question of who will play with him in the park now.

And now this. Adam, 18 years old, felt ashamed of failing his first Science exam. It shouldn't have been a big deal elsewhere, but he was at Princeton. He got there on pure merit, yet he didn't feel like he belonged there. He felt as if he was just lucky to be there. He had stayed up all those nights studying from Khan Academy and from Udemy courses that his average-rated high school couldn't teach, only to pull his family out of a continuous cycle of shut-down notices from the gas company, the electric company, and the water company. Now he realized why his father wouldn't let anyone open his daily mail. They were mostly shutdown notices. But now, at Princeton, he was dead scared of not belonging among the high rollers of talent and their quick-witted answers. His anxiety whipped up doubts about his own achievements so far.

Stories like these, the stories of anxiety and stress in children are so pervasive that it's no wonder we see so many *other* crises springing out of child stress and anxiety. The crisis of parent-child fighting, the crisis of runaway children, the crisis of child smoking, the crisis of opioid, the crisis of underage drinking, the crisis of self-harming, the crisis of complete silence and withdrawal. All these crises spring from the anxiety and stress that keep festering in our homes.

No wonder, the most common question concerned and stressed out parents ask of me these days is: how to deal with the stress and anxiety of their children. This not only affects the mental health of children, it also impacts the mental health of parents who must face the consequences of agitated, short-tempered, and belligerent children. It doesn't just stop at temper tantrums or shouting matches between parents and children. It often leads to total withdrawal, abandonment, or even self-harm if left go unchecked.

In this book, I will explore this grave issue of child and adolescent anxiety in depth. There are three parts to this analysis. In part I, I will explain what everyone must know about child emotions and child behaviors, whether you are a parent, a teacher, or a student counselor. In Part II, I will explore the most common reasons or triggers that cause anxiety and stress in children. And finally, in part III, I will recommend some strategies or solutions to manage these anxious and stressful behaviors. These strategies are directed both at parents as well as children.

Let's start with Part I.

Part I

Things Everyone Should Know About Child Emotions

The Three Scenarios

Meredith was a family friend. Chubby and sweet. Only she, among all others, would rarely ever bring Sarah, her teenage daughter, to our family-friends' get-togethers. While all others of her daughter's age played and chatted in our basement, her eyes would swell whenever Sarah's name came up in our *'how the kids are doing?'* conversations. No one pressed her any further. She called me one morning after. "Saleem, I wish I could also bring Sarah with me to play with other kids, but she always seems sad and refuses to go anywhere. She can't pinpoint any one thing that's making her this way. She gets more uncomfortable when she is around other friends."

Lauren worked with me until recently. She is now in another state. She was like one of those candid camera mommies. She would tell everybody everything that's going on at home. She would even share her kids' grades in school with everyone. She would laugh at every little oddity at work. Only I knew the pain she was hiding in her laughs. Her oldest son, Ralph, had cursed her so often in anger that she was now scared of him. He was ten inches taller even as a teen. He wouldn't care if the six-year old Liz hid in the coat closet when he was yelling at his mother. Thrice he had left home for days in anger and returned only when the police brought him home. And yet, there was no one thing Lauren could do to make Ralph a normal boy, just like all the other kids she knew about.

Ahmed had lived in our neighborhood two blocks over. His father, Jameel, was a friend of mine and his mother was my wife's friend. He went to high school with our son. He did just okay at school, like Bs and Cs etc. My son wasn't much of a good friend with him. Ahmed's friends were also just like him, all Bs and Cs kind. Often, they would loiter around the neighborhood huddled in one corner or the other. But as soon as they would see a familiar adult coming across, they would scurry away. People in the neighborhood knew me as a teacher preacher, the kind parents would send their kids to for a word of advice. But here was Ahmed, the son of a friend I couldn't talk to. I casually brought Ahmed's scurrying away up to Jameel one evening. He said, "It's not only with you. He is afraid of speaking to any adult who might ask him *'How are things going at school?'* He has some unknown fear of being called out." It wasn't just with me. It was with anyone who might ask him how he is doing. Jameel knew about Ahmed's fear of facing people, but he had no clue what to do about it. And things looked just okay with Ahmed, so he never worried too much about it.

So, what can we do about it?

Parents, like Meredith, Lauren, and Jameel are consumed by the struggles they have to put up with their growing children. There is no parenting school that teaches how to raise emotionally psychologically stable and successful children in the 21st century. All their parenting lives they keep throwing mud pies at the shifting goals of their kids' behaviors and hope some might stick. This is frustrating to see so many of their attempts at correcting their kids' behaviors have failed.

Let's help these parents with the first thing first: *Knowing the vocabulary of emotions and behaviors*. Just knowing in general that a kid is afraid, angry, or sad doesn't tell them much to get to the underlying triggers of such emotions. These are just general and vague categories. No wonder many of these kids themselves can't be specific as to what's bothering them. They don't have the vocabulary to tell what's going on inside of their heads. In this section we will go over the vocabulary of emotions that parents and children need to get familiar with before they can identify and isolate the causes of such emotions.

The following Emotions Wheel is a nice visual description of how to narrow down from a general category of emotions to a specific state of mind.

Credits: 9gag.com

This is a simple pinwheel chart that lists six basic emotions at its core. Take, for example, Sadness emotion at the center of the wheel. Sitting with your children and asking them to let you help them pinpoint whether this sadness is more like a feeling of abandonment, despair, or loneliness can narrow your search down to the third outermost layer of emotions. Let's say your child identifies a feeling of *Abandonment*, you can now ask if it is more like being *Ignored* or being *Victimized*. Once you get to this level of specific exploration of emotions with your child, you can identify who is ignoring or victimizing your child. Now you know the trigger that causes that sadness in your child.

Now, let's take Ralph's example above. He was always angry. If Lauren knew from the emotions wheel that anger could be a feeling of being constantly criticized, being frustrated, or being hated at school, she could have narrowed Ralph's feelings down to being a victim of constant sarcasm, irritation, or resentment. Now she would know why he remains angry all the time. Now she could do something about the instigators of such feelings.

And now, we will go over Ahmed's example above of being in constant fear. Looking at the emotions wheel above, we know fear could be categorized as insecurity, rejection, or humiliation. Ahmed's dad could have probed with his son to dig into the possible causes of these feelings. They could have been due to a sense of inferiority, insignificance, or ridicule, as seen in the outermost layer of the emotions wheel. Gaining Ahmed's confidence to open up and help him identify the real causes of his fear will help them both devise plans to counter the triggers of his fear.

I know full well it's easier said than done to say your child will open up to share with you the real feelings behind these emotions. That's why you must tame your expectations from any one single session with your child. This level of exploration of adolescent emotions requires a high level of trust with your child. And only a history of non-judgmental relationship with your child will offer you such an opportunity to sit with your child and discuss their deepest insecurities. If that history doesn't exist, either you find someone who has that kind of history with your child and train them on emotional literacy first, or reset your own relationship with your child over a period of time on the terms of non-judgment of their insufficiencies and failings before even attempting to probe them on the innermost layers of their feelings and emotions. This means you watch out what you say to your children and how you say it. No parent does it with mal-intention but many do mess up their relationships, just for the way they express their frustrations with them. Here are the things you don't say to your anxiety-ridden child and how to say them right:

1. *Stop worrying!*

   This command assumes your child is actively 'doing' worrying which he can 'stop doing' and their worries will go away. This means you are blaming your children for their condition. The best way is to say it this way. "Your worries are real. Let's do something about them. I want to make sure I am doing everything I need to do to help in this situation."

2. *You will be alright.*

Although true in many cases of temporary anxiety, it may backfire for your apparent disconnect with your child's pain. Unless you connect it with a similar experience in the past when your child did feel alright after some time, this comment will not have its desired effect. The best way to say it will be something like this. *"The last time it happened you were able to solve it this way. It seems different this time, but together we will find a way to solve it, but it may take some time before you start feeling better."*

3. *You are making it a big deal.*

It's a matter of perspective. From a child's perspective, their concern IS a big deal. It may not really be a big deal. But, before you invite them to look at something from your perspective, you have to acknowledge their perspective and echo it, "yes, it is a big deal." And after an appropriate pause, come back and say, "let's look at it another way." There will be a push back, but it won't be out of outright rejection. It will give you a keyhole to pry into.

4. *Stop thinking about it.*

   Before YOU even say it, THEY don't want to think about it. Yet, thinking about worries does not turn off and on like a switch. This is where the knowledge of emotions as shown in the emotions wheels earlier comes in handy. That helps you pinpoint what they really are thinking about. Are they thinking about an upcoming confrontation with a friend, or they are thinking about the embarrassment of a flunked test? Giving your child the confidence that you will be on their side when dealing with the fallout of upcoming fears, even when it's their fault, will help them overcome their thinking about it. Better yet, if they could write out the fallout and what you are going to do to deal with it will help them put their worries aside. Writing worries and their fallout helps take them out from their mind and onto a piece of paper. But this writing must be done in specifics, like, "If I am found responsible for lying in front of the principal about my friends, I will admit 'lying' and I will tell them I got scared of the consequences of being called out in front of my friends. But since now it's open I admit I told the untruth and I am ready for the consequences. I want to take this burden off my conscience and make a fresh start." People like admission of remorse because it shows a willingness to repair and a sign of reliability in future. Writing specifics like this is like staring down one's own demons.

5. *Forget it! I will do it myself.*

Quite often in your own hurry to get something done while your child is preoccupied with their own worries, you blurt out, "Forget it. I will do it myself." This drowns a child further deeper into anxiety stuck under the burden of their own worries and now added on to that your declaration they are of no good to you and to the family. Befriending your child in a way that you are aware of your child's preoccupation with their worries stops you from adding the double whammy of breaking expectations of their parents. Even if it's something that must be done timely, first make sure they are not being whacked with guilt when you must do something yourself. Acknowledge their preoccupation with their genuine worries first and then do yourself whatever needs to be done timely. But soon after, return to them and revisit their worries. This confirms you were not playing the 'guilt' card when you offered to do what THEY should have done in the first place.

Robert Plutchik's Wheel of Emotions

In another iteration of the wheel of emotions described earlier in this part, a pioneer in child psychology, Dr. Robert Plutchik (1927-2006) created the following floral-patterned wheel of emotions. He divided this flower into three circular patterns, from the smaller inner circle to the larger outer circle. The middle circle is the one where he laid the eight basic human emotions: *Joy, Trust, Fear, Surprise, Sadness, Disgust, Anger, and Anticipation.* The intensity of each of these emotions rises as we move towards the inner circles. The intensity of these emotions lowers as we move towards the outer circles on each petal. You would also notice the petals lying on the opposite side of each other have opposite emotions. Joy is the opposite of Sadness in the middle circle. Anger is opposite to Fear. Anticipation is the opposite of surprise. And in between any two petals there is a combination of emotions that exists in these two states. For example, Remorse is the result of Sadness and Disgust. Submission is the result of Trust and Fear.

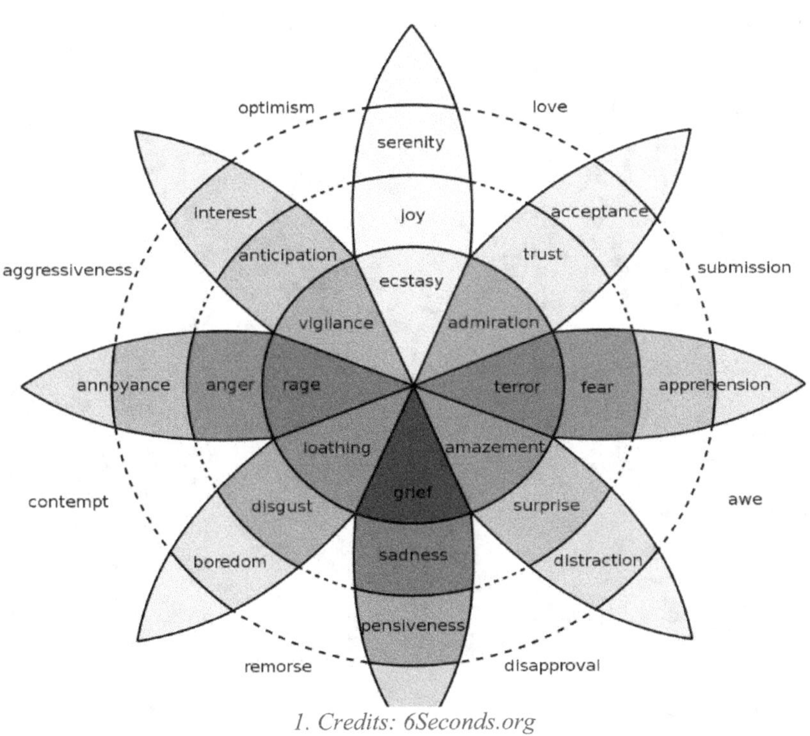

1. Credits: 6Seconds.org

The purpose of describing Robert Plutchik's wheel of emotions is not to make you a child psychologist, it's only to equip you with the knowledge of behaviors and emotions so you could identify and deal with the specific triggers that cause negative emotions.

Next, in Part II, we will go over the reasons and the triggers that most often cause child anxiety.

Part II

The Reasons and The Triggers Behind Child Anxieties

In this part, we will go over the triggers and reasons that often cause the most common anxieties and stress in children. We can generally categorize the triggers or causes of child anxiety into three broad categories, although there are so many more in addition to these three.

Fear of Failure

The Number One reason for anxiety and stress in children is the Fear of Failure. It's the fear of not meeting one's own expectations or the expectations of others around them. This fear could discourage a child from taking even the initial steps towards a given task or a goal, lest they should be considered a failure. In fact, it's not the actual failing, it's the impression or the perception of failure in front of others that would discourage a child from even trying a basketball throw, or try to balance oneself on skates, or to make a simple speech in front of their classmates. It's the anxiety of failing to meet the expectations of others that would deter a child from even participating in such activities. This is the fear of not being good enough. This is the debilitating paralysis of not being strong enough, not being rich enough, not being quick enough, not being smart enough to help others, or to help those they love. Trying to do any of this and failing at that could be devastating for a child's self-esteem. Not attempting at all, at least, will provide a safe exit or excuse: *"I didn't fail since I didn't even try."* And since society is more forgiving of quitters than of failures, it offers relatively generous face saving to quitters rather than to failures. The ones who attempt and fail have challenged the status quo, thus they must be met with rebuke, or censure, or dress down. Quitters, on the other hand, accept the status quo, hence they get a pass. But a pass from a situational embarrassment pushes them deeper into a depression hole of self-loathing, self-hating.

Fear of Rejection

The Number Two reason for anxiety and stress in children is the Fear of Rejection. It's the fear of rejection by one's existing or potential future friends. This fear presents itself due to the feeling of 'not being able to fit in.' It's the 'inner rivalry to fit in' with other friends. In this often-unspoken rivalry, children end up over-projecting themselves or undercutting their own friends, thus alienating those they are trying to win favors of. Those of us who follow reality TV shows witness these sorts of rivalries, jealousies, and feuds erupt even in those phony, staged settings.

Stigma

The Number Three category of reasons for anxiety and stress in children is Stigma. Stigmas that children face come in all forms and intensities. The stigma of looks, the stigma of body shapes, the stigma of financial or ethnic classes, the stigma of cultures, the stigma of the types of food they eat, the stigma of personal disabilities. All sorts of stigmas when exploited by others can lead to internalizing of anxiety, shame, helplessness, or resentment. Since there is little that children can do about these social or biological differences, they feel wronged by society or by their parents to have them put in these situations. Their anger pivots towards their being born in the wrong place, to the wrong parents. Notwithstanding the fact that all such stigmas are highly relative to each individual community. The stigma in one community could be a matter of pride in another. Fair-skinned in one society cherish the tanned-skinned in another. Being skinny in one place is deemed a sign of poverty or underfed, while in another it's a desirable body shape.

Here is the story of a stigma and a dilemma of a child who was born transgender. Her stubbornly denying parents sent her to a church-affiliated private school to give her the 'right nurturing fit for a man', where all the boys were supposed to grow up macho men, although she felt herself like a girl. You can well imagine her mental condition for all those years she had to endure the "right nurturing" to fix her by those macho boys. Stigmas like these can have a stunting effect on a child's mental and physical growth.

In this section, we have covered three major categories of triggers or sources of anxiety in children: The Fear of Failure, The Fear of Rejection, and The Stigma. This ends Part II of this book. In part III, I will go over some of the strategies and the solutions to counter or manage the effects of these debilitating sources of child anxiety.

Part III

The Solutions and The Strategies to Manage Child Anxiety

In part III of this book on child anxiety and stress, I will go over some of the strategies parents can use with their children in helping them overcome the debilitating effects of mild to moderate anxiety and stress. But before I start, let me start with these words from the famous psychologist, Steven Hayes. He says, *"If you always do what you've always done, you'll always get what you've always got."*

The first step in overcoming stubborn anxiety is the knowledge of what emotions are and how they work. Now the 'quick-to-conclusion' types among us will jump and say, "We know all about emotions. We know when we are sad, mad, angry, or disgusted." But the question is: does your child have the ability to differentiate between being *mad* and being *betrayed*? Can your child differentiate between being *angry* and being *judgmental*? Does your child have the ability to differentiate between being *sad* and being *abandoned*? Knowing emotions to this level of specificity can help pinpoint a specific cause and a trigger that initiated a particular phase of anxiety in your child. This level of awareness alone can provide a sense of empowerment from a vague 'I am mad, sad, or upset' to 'Sam embarrassed me for wearing worn-out shoes in front of Julie, with whom I was supposed to go out on a hike this weekend. And I didn't have money to buy new shoes." With this level of specificity, we can inch towards an action step--either to raise money from some source for new shoes or be straightforward with Julie and let her know you can't have new shoes until some time.

Walter Anderson, a renowned painter and writer said it succinctly: *"Nothing diminishes anxiety faster than action."*

The knowledge of specific emotions, or Emotional Literacy provides a path to action steps towards the source or sources of anxiety. And *Action* is the antidote of anxiety. Speaking of action brings me to my next recommendation in combating child anxiety. This is a recommendation of physical activity, especially if it's done together with your child. By physical activity, I mean intense, fast, cardio-type activity, like biking, running, dancing, wall or mountain climbing, soccer, or playing basketball. These types of intense physical exercises release endorphin hormones in the body. The euphoric excitement you feel after a run is due to this surge of endorphins. This feeling of excitement is also called runner's high. Regular intense exercise can easily overcome mild to moderate levels of anxiety and depression without any medication, only through the release of endorphins. Yet, at this point, I must note that medications, like Prozac and Xanax do have a role in mental health, but they should only be considered for severe conditions where urgent intervention is necessary, since they also have their addictive side-effects, leading to possible permanent dependency. You can practice learning about emotions with your children without being an expert psychologist. One way of teaching about emotions and the ways of expressing them is through engaging your children in *'How would you react?'* type of questions in real-life scenarios. Take examples of contentious emotional issues from the neighborhood, from the relatives, from the newspapers and ask your child what they would do in such situations. Explore different options of how to respond. This gives them practice on exploring more than one reaction to any given situation. They would understand the difference between knee-jerk reactions to emotional conflicts and their cool-headed alternatives. It's an effective way of empowering your children and making them understand that surrendering to emotions without being mindful of their causes is only for the untrained in the art and science of emotions.

But before you can explore such options together, you would need to overcome barriers in communicating with children. One major barrier to effective treatment of anxiety and stress in children is the lack of trust or communication between parents and children. Children find it difficult to open up to their parents for fear of being blamed for their own troubles, even when it's true. I am stressing on parents as the first line of defense against child anxiety, because it's the parents' life too which gets affected when their children are distressed. Now, in my experience, there are two things that I have found highly effective in building trust and communication with your child. I am saying this on the authority of a parent, who has recently raised three teenage boys with varying levels of success, but overall, I am pretty happy with the outcome. I must admit I had a great help in the form of their mother who was onboard with most of the recommendations I am making here. We often worked in tandem with each other in making sure there is consistency and continuity in the methods. This mention of teamwork brings me back to the one factor that contributes immensely to child anxiety and depression. And that is the factor of broken families in today's society. The absence of a father or a mother figure from the family CAN and WILL affect the sense of security and protection in children. Let me be clear here. Just the presence of a father or a mother around without an active positive engagement in children's life is like there being no father or no mother. Forced bonding by asking your child to sit with you or spend time with you, without piquing their curiosity to how they will benefit from spending time with you is of no consequence. Bonding with children comes in two ways. First, give them a judgment-free environment. They must be sure their parents will not judge them when they fail or falter. Their parents will come to their support even when they are wrong, especially in front of someone else. An unconditional judgment-free home does not mean a free-for-all absence of any accountability. It just means failure is accepted as an acceptable option when an effort is proven made towards a goal. Second chance, a third chance, even a fourth chance should always be an option as long informed decisions are made towards the tasks set before a child. Realignment, redirection, or even abandoning of certain goals should be clear options agreed upon ahead of time for every goal in life. That's bringing down the walls of judgment only parents can assist with. Another way authentic bonding with children can develop is by engaging them in authentic new learning. Empowering your child with new knowledge, new skills, or new learning provides a relationship of respect and curiosity. Curious children when they know they can gain valuable knowledge and skills from you would always come around to spend time with you. That calls for parents' own zeal for constant new learning of things. We are fortunate to be living in a day and age when new learning is so easily accessible. For starters,

Khan Academy, YouTube, Udemy offer a wealth of free resources on almost any topic. Learn something new and share it with your children. They may not display any interest in the beginning I must caution you. But a consistent regular sharing of whatever you learn on a variety of topics will develop into an atmosphere of meaningful and purposeful engagement with your children. Symbolic times together, like mealtime or game time, or even browsing time when combined with conversations revolving around new learning become the instances of cherishable 'quality time' spent together. If you want to up the notch for high-performing children, there are now formal and totally FREE courses available on any topic imaginable by some of the top universities in the world, like Harvard, Stanford, Princeton, Cambridge, Oxford, and so many more. Just Google search for Massive Online Open Courses, also called MOOCs and you will be surprised by the abundance of options available to gain that respect from your child that you had always wanted.

Now, here are some of the behaviors that as a parent you can model that your children will pick up over time. First up, model stress and emotional management through your own behavior. If you get louder during an argument, children will pick up and mimic that behavior. Being louder often means you are out of argument, patience, or respect with the other person. Displaying, or even initially faking an active listening composure in agitating situations or conversations, will lead to a lasting culture of listening to others' perspectives before countering them. We often hear things like, *"I gave her enough time before I got loud."* This is mere evasion. There is no such thing as a limit of time or trials before getting louder. If necessary, you can put a contentious topic to rest with your child for some time before taking it up again, without losing your calm composure. This particular advice also goes along with *'checking your ego'* in heated conversations. Many a time, in the heat of asserting your authority as a parent, you end up asserting your ego. Your goal is to gain their respect and have an influence on their decision making, not to inflict fear in them through your physical or financial authority. To check your ego, try saying *'sorry'* once in a while and notice a change in their behaviors. Expressing remorse or humility for a mistake made is a powerful trait of emotionally intelligent people. It's no weakness. In fact, it serves as the indirect influencing of permanent changes in stubborn behaviors. It produces softness in attitudes towards others. It brings down the rigid walls of defiance and insult. It fluffs the cushions of care from the very same people who were bent on pushing you down in the first place.

One of the best supports a parent can provide to their child is to make sure they get respected and accepted by their peers and their teachers. Empower your children to gain influence among their peers. Invite their friends to your house and make them feel welcome. This will bring down many of the cultural and social stigmas your children face at school. It will also help with the Fear of Rejection by their peers. This will also help them gain respect at school. Make frequent respectful contacts with your children's teachers and keep them in loop with all such communications. Remember you are advocating for your children, and not for their teacher. It's okay to offer alternatives that are acceptable to the teacher and your children, instead of blindly accepting the teacher's perspective. Teachers are human beings. They will listen to suggestions if offered with due deference.

The Last Word

There is no quick reset button to alter your child's state of anxiety or stress, just like there is no reset button to alter the essence of your relationship with your child. It's an accumulation of your interaction with your child from day one in every facet of life. It will take a long time to take the form you want your relationship to take with your child even if you decide to reset it today. So, parents' patience and perseverance are prerequisites towards this end. Since relationship building is a life-long endeavor, those who are unfamiliar with the art and science of emotions will forever flounder in their relationships, hence constantly dealing with bouts of anxiety and stress. But those who get trained in the science of emotions and behaviors early on in their lives thrive in their relationships. These are the people who become '*the wises*' in the family or who are considered balanced and stable in their relationships. They are the ones who earn the trust of those they are around.

And now this becomes the responsibility of the reader, YOU, to spread the word of this book early on to those who are just embarking on the journey of life. It's never too early or too late to talk about emotions and behaviors with your children, your siblings, your friends, your co-workers, or your parents.

Spread the good word!

About the Author

Dr. H. M. Saleem is an educator, a parent, and a trainer on instructional technology and emotional intelligence. This is his second book in two months. He has helped thousands of parents and teachers ride the roller coaster wave of emotional lockdown along with the real lockdown of this pandemic. He teaches how to harness the powers of instructional technology and thrive emotionally in these circumstances. He lives in New Jersey with his 'bride' and the three boys.